From Classroom to Law Firm: A Teacher's Guide to Becoming a Lawyer

By Silas Meadowlark

Index

- Deciding to Become a Lawyer
  - Evaluating Your Strengths and Interests
  - Understanding the Legal Profession
  - Weighing the Pros and Cons

- Navigating the Education Path
  - Pursuing an Undergraduate Degree
  - Choosing the Right Law School
  - Excelling in Law School

- Passing the Bar Exam
  - Preparing for the Bar Exam
  - Strategies for Success
  - Dealing with Exam Anxiety

- Building Practical Experience
  - Internships and Clerkships
  - Pro Bono Work
  - Networking and Mentorship

- Developing Essential Skills
  - Legal Research and Writing
  - Oral Advocacy and Presentation
  - Problem-Solving and Critical Thinking

- Transitioning to a Law Firm
  - Researching Law Firm Cultures
  - Crafting a Winning Resume and Cover Letter
  - Acing the Interview Process

- Navigating Law Firm Life
  - Understanding Billable Hours and Productivity
  - Work-Life Balance and Stress Management

- Continuing Professional Development

- Building a Successful Practice
  - Developing a Niche Expertise
  - Marketing and Client Development
  - Advancing to Partner or Counsel

- Specializing in a Legal Field
  - Corporate and Business Law
  - Litigation and Trial Practice
  - Family and Domestic Relations

- Exploring Alternative Career Paths
  - Government and Public Service
  - In-House Counsel
  - Legal Consulting and Entrepreneurship

- Overcoming Challenges and Setbacks
  - Dealing with Rejection and Failure
  - Maintaining Resilience and Perseverance
  - Seeking Support and Mentorship

- Balancing Work and Personal Life
  - Effective Time Management
  - Cultivating Hobbies and Interests
  - Maintaining Healthy Relationships

- Giving Back to the Community
  - Pro Bono Work and Volunteer Opportunities
  - Participating in Bar Associations
  - Mentoring and Educating Future Lawyers

- Adapting to a Changing Legal Landscape
  - Technological Advancements in the Legal Field
  - Emerging Areas of Law and Practice
  - Continuous Learning and Adaptation

- Leaving a Lasting Legacy
  - Reflections on a Rewarding Career

- Passing on Knowledge and Wisdom
- Retirement and Transition Planning

Deciding to Become a Lawyer

Evaluating Your Strengths and Interests

So, you're considering the legal profession? Well, buckle up, my friend, because it's a wild ride filled with endless possibilities and a few speed bumps along the way. But before you take the plunge, it's vital to do a little soul searching and figure out if this path is really for you.

First and foremost, ask yourself: what are your strengths and passions? Are you a natural born debater, able to argue your way out of a paper bag? Do you have a keen eye for detail and a knack for research? Or perhaps you're a master of persuasion, the kind of person who could convince a vegetarian to try a bacon wrapped steak (not that we're encouraging that, of course).

Seriously, though, take a good, long look at your skills and interests. Because let's face it, the legal world is a minefield of jargon, tedious paperwork, and enough stress to turn your hair gray overnight. You need to be the kind of person who thrives on challenge, who gets a glimmer in their eye when faced with a complex problem to untangle.

But don't worry, it's not all doom and gloom. The legal profession also offers incredible opportunities to make a real difference in people's lives, to be a voice for the voiceless, and to tackle some of the most pressing issues facing our society. If that lights a fire within you, then you might just have what it takes to become a true legal eagle.

Understanding the Legal Profession

Alright, let's dive a little deeper into the world of law and what it really means to be a lawyer. It's not all fancy courtroom dramas and high powered negotiations, you know. In fact, the day to-day grind can be downright mundane at times.

Picture this: you're hunched over your desk, surrounded by a mountain of case files, your eyes burning from staring at the computer screen for hours on end. Your coffee's gone cold, and you're pretty sure you've forgotten what the sun looks like. But then, that moment of triumph when you uncover a critical piece of evidence or craft the perfect legal strategy – that's the stuff that keeps lawyers going, that sense of accomplishment and the thrill of the chase.

And let's not forget the importance of networking and building relationships in the legal field. It's not just about your legal skills; it's also about your ability to navigate the often complex web of professional connections, to schmooze with potential clients, and to keep your name at the top of everyone's mind.

But hey, don't let that intimidate you. With the right mindset and a healthy dose of perseverance, you can thrive in this high powered world. Just be prepared to put in the hard work, stay curious, and never stop learning. Because in the legal profession, the only constant is change.

Weighing the Pros and Cons

Alright, let's get real – becoming a lawyer isn't all sunshine and rainbows. There's a lot to consider, and it's important to weigh the pros and cons carefully before taking the leap.

On the plus side, the legal field offers a level of prestige and respect that can be hard to come by in other professions. Plus, the earning potential is pretty darn impressive, with top tier lawyers raking in the big bucks. And let's not forget the intellectual challenge – solving complex problems and navigating the ever evolving terrain of the law can be incredibly rewarding.

But hold on to your gavel, folks, because there are also some serious downsides to consider. The workload can be crushing, with long hours, tight deadlines, and an endless stream of paperwork that could make even the most organized person cry tears of despair. And let's not forget the stress – the pressure to perform, the fear of making a costly mistake, and the constant need to stay on top of the latest legal developments.

Oh, and did we mention the student loan debt? Yep, that's a whole other can of worms. Sinking tens of thousands of dollars into a legal education is no joke, and it can take years to dig yourself out of that financial hole.

So, is the legal profession worth it? Well, that's a decision only you can make. But one thing's for sure – it's not a path for the faint of heart. If you're ready to embrace the challenges, thrive on pressure, and relish the opportunity to make a real impact, then the legal field might just be your calling. But if the thought of working 80 hour weeks and living on a steady diet of caffeine and anxiety makes you want to run for the hills, then maybe it's time to explore a different career path.

Navigating the Education Path

Pursuing an Undergraduate Degree

Beginning on the journey to becoming a lawyer begins with choosing the right undergraduate degree. The good news is, there is no one size-fits all approach. Law schools welcome applicants from a wide range of academic backgrounds, from English literature to engineering. The key is to select a program that coordinates with your interests and strengths, while also honing the critical thinking, communication, and analytical skills that are essential for legal practice.

As you explore your undergraduate options, consider coursework that challenges you to tackle complex problems, craft persuasive arguments, and think outside the box. Courses in philosophy, political science, history, and even the sciences can all provide a solid foundation for the rigors of law school. Don't be afraid to step outside your comfort zone and explore interdisciplinary studies – the more diverse your academic experiences, the better prepared you'll be to tackle the many-sided challenges of the legal field.

Alongside your coursework, be sure to take advantage of extracurricular opportunities that allow you to develop leadership, public speaking, and teamwork skills. Participate in mock trial competitions, join the debate team, or volunteer with local organizations. These experiences will not only improve your application but also provide valuable observations into the realities of the legal profession.

Remember, your undergraduate journey is about more than just securing a high GPA. It's about cultivating the intellectual curiosity, critical thinking, and problem solving abilities that will serve you well in law school and beyond. Embrace the opportunities to explore, challenge yourself, and discover the path that syncs best with your unique talents and aspirations.

Choosing the Right Law School

Selecting the right law school is a vital decision that can have a lasting impact on your career. While rankings and prestige are often the first factors that come to mind, it's essential to look beyond the surface and find a program that truly matches with your goals and learning style.

Start by reflecting on your priorities – do you want to specialize in a particular area of law? Are you interested in pursuing public service or working in a large corporate firm? Consider the strengths and specializations of each law school, as well as the opportunities they offer for practical experience, such as clinics, externships, and specialized concentrations.

Don't forget to factor in the school's culture and environment. Visit the campuses, attend information sessions, and speak with current students to get a sense of the community. Is the atmosphere collaborative or competitive? Are there opportunities for mentorship and support? These intangible factors can greatly influence your overall law school experience and your transition into the legal profession.

Equally important is the financial aspect of your law school decision. Carefully research tuition, cost of living, and scholarship opportunities. While the price tag shouldn't be the sole determining factor, it's important to understand the long term implications of your choice and how it may impact your financial future. Weigh the potential return on investment against your career goals and personal financial situation.

Ultimately, choosing the right law school is a deeply personal decision that requires careful consideration of your unique needs and aspirations. Trust your instincts, do your research, and don't be afraid to think outside the box. The right program will not only prepare you for the challenges of the legal field but also provide the foundation for a rewarding and fulfilling career.

Excelling in Law School

Congratulations, you've made it to law school! Now the real work begins. Law school is undoubtedly a challenging and demanding experience, but with the right mindset and strategies, you can thrive in this academic environment.

First and foremost, embrace the unique teaching methods of law school, such as the Socratic method. Rather than passively absorbing information, you'll be expected to engage in lively discussions, defend your positions, and think on your feet. Approach each class with an open and curious mindset, ready to dive deep into the nuances of legal reasoning and analysis.

Time management and organization will be your best friends

in law school. Develop a system that works for you, whether it's color coding your notes, using digital tools to keep track of deadlines, or carving out dedicated study time. Remember, the workload can be overwhelming, but with effective strategies, you can stay on top of your game.

Networking and building strong relationships with your professors and peers should also be a priority. Engage in study groups, participate in extracurricular activities, and seek out mentors who can provide guidance and support. These connections can not only enrich your learning experience but also open doors to valuable opportunities, such as internships and research projects.

As you navigate the rigors of law school, don't forget to take care of yourself. Maintaining a healthy work life balance, managing stress, and finding ways to recharge are essential for your well being and academic success. Whether it's taking a break to exercise, practicing mindfulness, or simply spending time with loved ones, make self care a non negotiable part of your routine.

Finally, remember that excelling in law school is not just about achieving academic excellence. It's about honing the critical thinking, communication, and problem solving skills that will serve you well in the legal profession. Embrace the challenge, trust your abilities, and be willing to step outside your comfort zone. The journey may be demanding, but the rewards of becoming a lawyer are truly unparalleled.

Passing the Bar Exam

Preparing for the Bar Exam

Passing the bar exam is no easy feat, but with the right preparation, you can conquer this hurdle and take the first step towards your legal career. The key is to approach the exam with a strategic mindset and a persistent work ethic. First and foremost, dive deep into the exam format and content. Familiarize yourself with the structure, question types, and subject areas tested. This will help you develop a tailored study plan that maximizes your chances of success.

Now, let's talk about the study materials. Forget the one size-fits all approach - you need to curate a personalized toolkit that caters to your learning style. Explore a variety of resources, from practice questions and flashcards to comprehensive review courses and study groups. Don't be afraid to experiment and find what works best for you. And remember, consistency is key. Dedicate a substantial amount of time each day to reviewing, practicing, and reinforcing the material.

But it's not all about the books and the practice tests. Self care is just as vital during this intense preparation period. Maintain a healthy work life balance, get enough rest, and find ways to manage stress. Incorporate physical activity, mindfulness exercises, and social connections to keep your mind and body in peak condition. After all, you'll need to be at your best when facing the pressure cooker environment of the bar exam.

Strategies for Success

Acing the bar exam is like solving a complex puzzle - you need to have a well thought-out strategy to put all the pieces together. Start by mastering the art of time management. Develop a study schedule that allows you to cover all the topics thoroughly, while also leaving room for breaks and review sessions. Prioritize your weaknesses and allocate more time to the areas that need the most attention.

Next, hone your test taking skills. Practice, practice, practice. Familiarize yourself with the types of questions you'll encounter, and learn techniques to tackle them efficiently. Develop a systematic approach to reading and analyzing the prompts, identifying the key issues, and crafting comprehensive responses. Don't underestimate the power of practice exams - they'll help you identify and address any gaps in your knowledge or test taking abilities.

As you examine deeper into your preparation, stay vigilant for shifts in the exam's content or format. Legal education and the legal profession are constantly evolving, so be sure to stay up to-date on any changes that may impact the bar exam. Adapt your study plan accordingly, and don't be afraid to seek guidance from experienced mentors or bar exam experts. Remember, the bar exam is a marathon, not a sprint, so pace yourself and trust the process.

Dealing with Exam Anxiety

Let's face it, the bar exam is a nerve wracking experience, even for the most seasoned law students. Anxiety can creep in, threatening to sabotage all the hard work you've put in. But fear not, there are strategies to help you manage those jitters and stay focused on the task at hand.

First and foremost, practice relaxation techniques. Deep breathing exercises, meditation, and visualization can do wonders for calming your mind and body. Experiment with different methods and find what works best for you. Incorporate these practices into your daily routine, not just on the day of the exam.

Positive self talk is also essential. Replace those inner doubts with affirmations of confidence and capability. Remind yourself of your strengths, your preparation, and your unwavering determination. Surround yourself with a support system of family, friends, and mentors who can bolster your spirits and provide encouragement when the going gets tough.

Finally, don't forget to take care of your physical well being. Proper nutrition, adequate sleep, and regular exercise can help you manage stress and stay energized throughout the exam. Avoid last minute cramming and instead, focus on maintaining a healthy routine. Remember, the bar exam is a marathon, not a sprint, so pace yourself and trust that your preparation will pay off.

Building Practical Experience

Internships and Clerkships

Ah, the age old question - how do you get that elusive "experience" when every job listing demands it like a hungry wolf howling at the moon? The answer, my friend, lies in the power of internships and clerkships. These hidden gems are your ticket to breaking into the legal world, and trust me, they're worth their weight in gold plated gavels.

First up, internships. These little slices of professional paradise are like a fast track to real world expertise. Think of it as a legal version of "try before you buy" - you get to dip your toes into different areas of practice, rub elbows with seasoned attorneys, and discover whether your true calling lies in corporate contracts or family law. And the best part? You don't even need to worry about the dreaded "no experience required" curse - internships are designed to help you build that all important foundation.

Now, clerkships - these are the legal equivalent of a VIP backstage pass. As a clerk, you'll have the unique opportunity to work alongside a judge, observing the inner workings of the judicial system and honing your legal research and writing skills. It's like a crash course in judicial decision making, and trust me, there's nothing quite like it. Plus, the networking potential is off the charts - judges have a knack for remembering the sharp, hardworking clerks who've graced their chambers.

Whether you choose an internship or a clerkship (or, hey, why not both?), the key is to approach these experiences with the enthusiasm of a golden retriever and the focus of a laser guided missile. Soak up every bit of knowledge, volunteer for every project, and don't be afraid to ask questions - the more you put in, the more you'll get out.

Pro Bono Work

Let's talk about pro bono work, the unsung hero of the legal world. While the glitz and glamour of high profile cases might seem like the ultimate goal, it's the pro bono work that truly sets the trailblazers apart. Think of it as the secret sauce that adds a touch of magic to your career.

Sure, it might not come with a hefty paycheck, but the rewards are priceless. By dedicating your time and skills to those in need, you'll not only be making a tangible difference in people's lives, but you'll also be building a reputation as a compassionate, community minded legal eagle. And let's not forget the networking potential - working alongside other pro bono superstars is like a master class in professional connections.

But it's not all altruism and warm fuzzies - pro bono work can also be a powerful tool in honing your legal skills. From navigating complex bureaucratic systems to mastering the art of persuasive writing, every pro bono case is a chance to sharpen your abilities and expand your expertise. And let's be honest, there's nothing quite like the satisfaction of helping someone navigate the often daunting legal scene and emerge victorious.

So, don't be afraid to dive headfirst into the world of pro bono work. Whether it's volunteering at a local legal clinic or taking on a special project for a non profit organization, the opportunities are endless. Trust me, your future self will thank you for the experience, the connections, and the pure, unadulterated joy of making a difference.

Networking and Mentorship

Alright, let's talk about the secret sauce of legal success: networking and mentorship. These two dynamic duo are the keys to making accessible doors, forging powerful connections, and soaring to new heights in your legal career.

First up, networking. It's not just about handing out business cards and making small talk - it's about building genuine relationships with people who can help you grow, both personally and professionally. Think of it as a legal version of speed dating, except instead of finding your soulmate, you're searching for your next big break.

Attend industry events, volunteer for bar association committees, or even strike up conversations with fellow lawyers at the courthouse coffee shop. You never know where that next opportunity might come from. And don't forget the power of online networking - LinkedIn is like a virtual cocktail party, so get out there and start mingling.

But networking is only half the battle - the real game changer is finding a mentor. These seasoned legal eagles are like the Yodas of the profession, ready to share their hard earned wisdom and guide you through the treacherous waters of the legal world. Whether it's a partner at your firm or a respected judge in your community, a good mentor can be the difference between treading water and swimming with the sharks.

Seek out potential mentors at professional events, or reach out directly and ask if they'd be willing to share their expertise. Be prepared to listen, learn, and put their advice into action. And remember, the mentor mentee relationship is a two way street - be sure to give back by offering your own unique perspectives and skills.

So, get out there, network like a pro, and find yourself a mentor who can help you navigate the legal world with the grace of a figure skater and the tenacity of a pit bull. Trust me, your career will thank you.

Developing Essential Skills

Legal Research and Writing

As a teacher turned-lawyer, you'll quickly realize that the ability to conduct thorough legal research and craft compelling written arguments is the backbone of your new profession. It's time to bid farewell to the days of crafting captivating lesson plans and hello to the world of convoluted case law and meticulous citation formats. But fear not, my fellow academic warriors - with the right strategies and a healthy dose of caffeine, you'll be churning out legal masterpieces that would make even the most seasoned litigator green with envy.

The key to effective legal research is to approach it with the same tenacity and curiosity that you brought to the classroom. Forget about browsing through outdated textbooks; you'll be delving into the depths of online databases, scouring through endless digital archives, and uncovering case law that would make even the most seasoned detective green with envy. But don't get too caught up in the thrill of the hunt - remember, the ultimate goal is to find that elusive piece of information that will give your argument the winning edge.

And when it comes to legal writing, it's time to say goodbye to the flowery prose and creative metaphors that once graced your lesson plans. In the world of law, precision and clarity reign supreme. Your writing must be concise, well structured, and meticulously referenced, with a keen eye for detail that would make even the most detecting English professor nod in approval. But fear not, my wordy warrior - with practice and a willingness to embrace the art of brevity, you'll be crafting legal documents that would make even the most seasoned partner swoon.

Oral Advocacy and Presentation

If you thought standing in front of a classroom of fidgety students was nerve wracking, just wait until you find yourself standing before a judge, a jury, or a room full of skeptical partners. But fear not, my eloquent educator, for your years of honing your public speaking skills have prepared you for this very moment.

The key to effective oral advocacy is to approach it with the same level of passion and charisma that you brought to the classroom. Gone are the days of dry, monotonous lectures; now, you'll be captivating your audience with the power of your words, the force of your arguments, and the sheer force of your personality. Embrace your inner thespian and let your passion for the law shine through in every word, every gesture, and every subtle nuance of your delivery.But don't just rely on your natural charm and wit - hone your skills through practice, practice, and more practice. Rehearse your arguments until they're seared into your memory, and be prepared to think on your feet when the unexpected inevitably occurs. After all, you've dealt with the unpredictable before - just imagine your courtroom as a classroom filled with the most challenging students you've ever encountered, and you'll be well on your way to becoming a master of oral advocacy.

Problem Solving and Critical Thinking

As a teacher, you've already mastered the art of critical thinking and problem solving - after all, navigating the ever changing terrain of education is a challenge in and of itself. But now, you'll be putting those skills to the test in an entirely new arena: the legal profession.

Gone are the days of simple lesson planning and classroom management; now, you'll be tackling complex legal problems, analyzing elaborate case law, and devising creative strategies to outsmart the opposition. But fear not, my analytical alchemist, for your years of experience in the classroom have prepared you for this very moment.

Approach each legal challenge with the same level of curiosity and determination that you brought to the classroom. Dig deep, ask probing questions, and never be satisfied with the obvious answer. Channel your inner detective and uncover the hidden nuances, the unexpected twists, and the game changing realizations that will give your case the edge it needs. And when the pressure is on, remember to stay calm, cool, and collected - after all, you've handled far more chaotic situations than this in your teaching career.

Transitioning to a Law Firm

Researching Law Firm Cultures

Alright, future lawyers, listen up! When it comes to landing that dream job at a law firm, the secret sauce isn't just about your killer resume and interview skills (although those certainly help). Nope, the real key is understanding the firm's culture and how you'll fit into it. Think of it like finding your soulmate - except instead of Netflix and chill, you'll be diving headfirst into a world of billable hours, client meetings, and office politics.

Start by doing your homework, my friends. Scour the firm's website, social media pages, and any news articles about them. Pay close attention to the language they use, the types of clients they serve, and the values they claim to uphold. Are they all about that cutthroat, high stakes litigation vibe, or do they prefer a more collaborative, work life balance approach? Once you've got a feel for their DNA, it's time to put on your detective hat and dig deeper.

Reach out to your network - maybe that cousin who's been practicing law for a decade, or that random LinkedIn connection you made at a networking event. Pick their brains about the firm's reputation, work culture, and even the dreaded "billable hours" expectations. The more intel you can gather, the better equipped you'll be to assess whether this firm is truly the right fit for your unique skills and career aspirations.

And let's not forget the all important informational interview. Snag a chat with someone who's currently working at the firm, and you'll get an insider's perspective that no amount of online research can replicate. Ask about the day to-day, the challenges they face, and the type of support (or lack thereof) they receive from the firm's leadership. Trust me, this intel will be gold when it comes time to craft your "why this firm" pitch.

Crafting a Winning Resume and Cover Letter

Alright, future legal eagles, it's time to put your writing skills to the test. Crafting a killer resume and cover letter is the first step in catching the eye of that elusive law firm you've got your sights set on. But before you start frantically typing away, take a deep breath and remember: this isn't just about regurgitating your entire life story. Nope, it's about strategically showcasing your most relevant skills and experiences in a way that makes you stand out from the competition.

First up, the resume. Ditch the generic template and create a document that's as unique as you are. Use strategic formatting, eye catching section headers, and a clean, professional layout to make it easy for the reader to quickly digest your qualifications. And don't just list your responsibilities - highlight your accomplishments and the tangible impact you've made. Trust me, that's the stuff that'll make the hiring manager sit up and take notice.

Now, the cover letter. This is your chance to really let your personality shine through and make a personal connection with the reader. Start strong with a compelling opening that grabs their attention, then weave in a narrative that showcases your passion for the firm, your relevant skills, and why you'd be the perfect addition to their team. But don't just regurgitate what's on your resume - use this space to share something unique and memorable about yourself.

The key to crafting a winning resume and cover letter? Authenticity, my friends. Don't just tell them what you think they want to hear - show them who you truly are and why you'd be an essential asset to the firm. And remember, attention to detail is everything. Proofread, proofread, and proofread some more. After all, you wouldn't want a silly typo to be the reason you miss out on your dream job, would you?

Acing the Interview Process

Congratulations, future lawyer! You've made it past the first hurdle and landed an interview at your dream law firm. Now, it's time to put on your best poker face and show them why you're the total package. But don't worry, with a little preparation and a whole lot of confidence, you've got this in the bag.

First and foremost, research the heck out of the firm. Seriously, you should know their history, practice areas, and key players like the back of your hand. But don't just regurgitate facts - use that intel to demonstrate your genuine interest and enthusiasm for the firm. Drop a few strategic name drops, and maybe even reference a recent case or client that caught your eye. Trust me, they'll be impressed.

Next, get ready to showcase your legal chops. Anticipate the tough questions they might throw your way and have a few well crafted responses ready to go. Can you analyze a complex legal issue, identify the key challenges, and propose a solid solution? Heck yeah, you can! And don't forget to sprinkle in some of those essential lawyering skills, like critical thinking, problem solving, and the ability to think on your feet.

But let's not forget the all important personal touch. Remember, these folks aren't just looking for a legal eagle - they want someone who's going to mesh well with the team and contribute to the firm's unique culture. So, be ready to share a bit about your hobbies, interests, and even your quirky personality traits. After all, what's the point of landing your dream job if you can't have a little fun along the way?

And when the interview wraps up, don't forget to follow up with a killer thank you note. This is your chance to reiterate your enthusiasm, highlight a few key points you discussed, and maybe even include a personal touch that'll make you stand out from the crowd. Trust me, a little bit of effort can go a long way in sealing the deal.

Navigating Law Firm Life

Understanding Billable Hours and Productivity

Welcome to the high octane world of law firm life, where the ticking clock is your constant companion and billable hours are the currency that fuels your career. As a former teacher beginning on your legal journey, prepare to bid farewell to the leisurely pace of the classroom and embrace a new reality where every minute counts.

Billable hours are the lifeblood of a law firm, and your proficiency in managing them will be a demonstration to your value. Forget about those cozy afternoons spent grading papers – in the legal realm, it's all about maximizing your productivity and squeezing every ounce of billable time out of each day. It's a delicate dance, my friend, where you must balance the need for accuracy and attention to detail with the constant pressure to bill, bill, bill.

But fear not, for with a little finesse and a lot of caffeine, you can conquer the billable hour beast. Develop laser sharp time management skills, learn to optimize your workflow, and become a master of efficient research and writing. Embrace the power of technology – those fancy legal research tools and document automation software will become your new best friends. And don't be afraid to delegate, delegate, delegate. Remember, you're part of a team, and delegating tasks can not only boost your productivity but also nurture the growth of junior associates.

Of course, the pursuit of billable hours can be a double edged sword. It's easy to get caught up in the rat race and forget the true purpose of our profession – serving our clients with integrity and passion. Resist the temptation to sacrifice quality for quantity, and always strive to deliver exceptional work. After all, what good are those impressive billable numbers if they're built on a foundation of sloppy legal work?

Work Life Balance and Stress Management

As a former teacher, you're no stranger to the demands of a high stakes profession. But the legal world has a way of pushing the boundaries of work life balance, testing the limits of even the most resilient individuals. It's a delicate tightrope walk, my friend, and one that requires constant vigilance and a healthy dose of self care.

The long hours, the endless deadlines, the pressure to always be "on" – it can all take a toll on your mental and physical well being. But fear not, for you possess a superpower that many of your legal counterparts may have forgotten: the art of work life balance. As a former teacher, you've honed the ability to prioritize self care and maintain your sanity in the face of daunting challenges.

Embrace your inner zen master and carve out time for yourself, even if it's just a few minutes each day. Take a brisk walk, indulge in a hobby that brings you joy, or simply sit in silence and breathe. Remember, your well being is not a luxury – it's a necessity, and it will fuel your success in the long run.

And when the stress starts to creep in, don't be afraid to reach out. Build a support network of trusted colleagues, mentors, and mental health professionals who can provide guidance and a listening ear. Lean on your law firm's resources, such as employee assistance programs and wellness initiatives, to help you navigate the challenges of this high intensity career path.

By prioritizing your well being and striking a healthy balance between work and personal life, you'll not only thrive in the legal profession but also inspire others to do the same. After all, a happy and healthy lawyer is a more effective lawyer – and that's a win win for everyone involved.

Continuing Professional Development

Congratulations, you've made it through the gauntlet of law school, passed the bar exam, and landed your dream job at a prestigious law firm. But don't rest on your laurels just yet, my friend – the journey of a lawyer is a never ending quest for knowledge and growth.

In the fast paced world of law, the legal terrain is constantly evolving, with new regulations, technologies, and standards emerging at a dizzying pace. To stay ahead of the curve and cement your reputation as a trusted advisor, you must embrace a mindset of continuous learning and professional development.

Carve out time in your schedule for ongoing education, whether it's attending industry conferences, participating in in house training programs, or pursuing specialized certifications. Keep your finger on the pulse of the latest legal trends, dive deep into emerging areas of practice, and continuously refine your skills in areas like legal research, writing, and advocacy.

But professional development isn't just about formal training – it's also about cultivating a diverse network of mentors, peers, and industry experts who can provide valuable perceptions and guidance. Seek out seasoned lawyers who have walked the path before you, and don't be afraid to pick their brains. Attend local bar association events, join professional organizations, and engage in peer to-peer learning opportunities to expand your horizons and stay ahead of the curve.

Remember, the true mark of a successful lawyer is not just their technical prowess, but their ability to adapt, innovate, and continuously evolve. By embracing a culture of lifelong learning and professional development, you'll not only future proof your career but also position yourself as a valuable asset to your law firm and your clients.

Building a Successful Practice

Developing a Niche Expertise

In the ever evolving legal situation, carving out a niche for yourself is the key to standing out from the crowd. Sure, you could be a jack of-all trades, but trust me, that's a fast track to becoming a master of none. Instead, dive deep into a specific area of the law and become the go to expert. It might seem daunting at first, but think of it this way – when was the last time you called your dentist for legal advice?

Now, I know what you're thinking – "But what if I'm interested in a dozen different areas?" Well, my friend, that's where the fun begins. Start by identifying the intersections, the sweet spots where your passions collide. Maybe you're fascinated by the intersection of intellectual property and the ever changing world of social media. Or perhaps you're drawn to the elaborate dance of corporate mergers and acquisitions. Whatever it is, embrace your inner geek and dive in headfirst.

Once you've found your niche, it's time to become the Yoda of that particular field. Attend industry conferences, join relevant professional associations, and make yourself an indispensable resource. Publish articles, give seminars, and position yourself as the go to expert. Trust me, clients will start beating down your door, and before you know it, you'll be the one setting the trends, not just following them.

Marketing and Client Development

Alright, let's talk about the not so-fun part of running a law practice – marketing and client development. I know, I know, it's not exactly the reason you became a lawyer, but trust me, it's a necessary evil. And if you do it right, it can actually be kind of fun.

First and foremost, ditch the stuffy, corporate speak marketing tactics. We're talking about building relationships here, not selling used cars. Instead, focus on being authentic, approachable, and genuinely interested in the needs of your clients. Think of it like a first date – you're not just trying to impress them with your credentials, you're trying to figure out if you're a good fit.

And speaking of first dates, let's talk about social media. Gone are the days of stuffy firm websites and outdated brochures. These days, your online presence is your calling card. So, get creative! Start a blog, share your expertise on LinkedIn, or even dabble in the wild world of TikTok. Just make sure you're providing value, not just shouting into the void.

But don't forget the good old fashioned face to-face networking. Attend industry events, join local bar associations, and get out there and mingle. You never know when that casual conversation at the hors d'oeuvres table might lead to your next big client. And don't be afraid to get a little quirky – I once landed a major contract by challenging the CEO to a heated debate about the merits of truffle oil. (Spoiler alert: I won.)

Advancing to Partner or Counsel

Alright, let's talk about the brass ring - making partner or becoming a sought after counsel. It's the dream, right? The ultimate goal? Well, buckle up, my friend, because the path to the top is no walk in the park.

First and foremost, you've got to be a rainmaker. I'm talking about bringing in clients like your life depends on it. And I'm not just talking about the occasional referral - I'm talking about building a steady stream of new business that keeps the firm humming. That means networking like a pro, pitching your services to potential clients, and always keeping an ear to the ground for the next big opportunity.

But it's not just about the numbers, you know. You've also got to be a superstar in the courtroom or the boardroom. Hone your legal skills to a razor sharp edge, become an expert in your field, and never stop learning. Attend conferences, take on challenging cases, and always be looking for ways to expand your knowledge and expertise.

And let's not forget about leadership. At the end of the day, partners and counsel aren't just legal powerhouses - they're also the ones steering the ship. So, get involved in firm management, volunteer for key committees, and start thinking like a leader. Show your colleagues and superiors that you've got the vision, the drive, and the strategic chops to take the firm to new heights.

Now, I'm not going to sugarcoat it - the path to the top is a tough one. There will be setbacks, long hours, and plenty of competition. But if you're up for the challenge, the rewards can be truly spectacular. So, roll up your sleeves, sharpen your elbows, and get ready to take the legal world by storm. The corner office is waiting, my friend – all you've got to do is reach out and grab it.

Specializing in a Legal Field

Corporate and Business Law

So, you've decided to ditch the classroom and dive headfirst into the high stakes world of corporate law? Buckle up, my friend, because this is a wild ride. While the corporate and business law realm may seem like a bastion of buttoned up suits and endless spreadsheets, trust me, there's a whole lot of excitement waiting for you.

First and foremost, you'll need to develop a keen eye for detail – the kind that can spot a loophole a mile away. Think of yourself as a legal Sherlock Holmes, scouring contracts and financial statements for any potential landmines. But don't just stop there – you'll also need to be a strategic mastermind, crafting airtight deals that not only protect your clients but also help them achieve their loftiest ambitions.

And let's not forget the art of negotiation. In the corporate world, it's a delicate dance of compromise and concession, where a single misplaced word can derail an entire transaction. You'll need to be a silver tongued orator, capable of wielding your words like a samurai wields their sword, slicing through the opposition's arguments with ease.

But the true thrill of corporate law lies in the high stakes, high pressure situations you'll find yourself in. Imagine standing in a boardroom, surrounded by the titans of industry, as you present a merger proposal that could make or break a client's empire. It's like a game of corporate chess, where every move you make could have colossal consequences.

And let's not forget the perks - the corner office with the sweeping city views, the lavish client dinners at Michelin starred restaurants, the feeling of power and influence that comes with being the legal mastermind behind some of the biggest deals in the business world. It's a life of luxury, excitement, and intellectual challenge, all wrapped up in a crisp, tailored suit.

So, if you're ready to trade in your whiteboard markers for a briefcase and a stack of legal pads, then corporate and business law might be the path for you. Just remember to pack your negotiation skills, your attention to detail, and your love of high stakes drama - because this is a world where every victory is hard fought, and the stakes are always sky high.

Litigation and Trial Practice

Ah, the world of litigation and trial practice - where the courtroom is your stage, and the truth is the ultimate weapon. If you're the type who thrives on adrenaline, craves the thrill of battle, and has a burning passion for justice, then this might just be the legal specialization for you.

Picture this: you're standing before a judge and jury, your pulse quickening as you deliver a blistering cross examination that leaves the opposing counsel scrambling. You've spent weeks poring over case files, meticulously building your argument, and now it's showtime. The stakes are high, the tension is palpable, and the only thing standing between your client and victory is your razor sharp wit and unshakable determination.

But it's not just about the courtroom drama – being a successful litigator requires a many-sided skill set. You'll need to be a master of legal research, digging through piles of evidence and precedents to uncover the key facts that will turn the tide in your favor. And let's not forget the art of persuasion – the ability to craft a compelling narrative that appeals with even the most skeptical of audiences.

And let's not forget the high stakes nature of this field. In the world of litigation, the stakes are never low. A single misstep, a single piece of overlooked evidence, could mean the difference between victory and defeat – between your client walking free or facing the harsh consequences of a loss. It's a pressure cooker environment, but for those who thrive on it, it's the ultimate adrenaline rush.

But the rewards of a career in litigation and trial practice go beyond the courtroom drama. You'll have the chance to make a real difference in people's lives, to be the advocate for for those who have been wronged, and to play a vital role in upholding the rule of law. It's a career where your skills and dedication can truly change the course of someone's life – and that's a legacy worth fighting for.

So, if you're ready to don your figurative legal armor, sharpen your rhetorical skills, and dive headfirst into the high stakes world of litigation and trial practice, then this might just be the path for you. Just be prepared to leave your comfort zone at the door, because in this field, the only constant is the thrill of the chase.

Family and Domestic Relations

Ah, the world of family and domestic relations law – where the heart meets the letter of the law. If you're the type who thrives on the emotional complexities of human relationships, and you have a deep well of empathy and compassion, then this might just be the legal specialization for you.

Picture yourself as the steadfast guide for families navigating the turbulent waters of divorce, child custody battles, and complex domestic disputes. You'll be the shoulder to lean on, the voice of reason in the midst of the storm, and the advocate for for the rights and well being of your clients and their loved ones.

But make no mistake, this is no easy path. Family and domestic relations law is a delicate and often heart wrenching field, where the stakes are high and the emotions can run deeper than the Pacific Ocean. You'll need to be a master of diplomacy, able to navigate the treacherous terrain of familial dynamics with the grace and tact of a seasoned diplomat.

And let's not forget the legal acumen required. You'll need to be a virtuoso of the Family Code, a ninja in the realm of child support calculations, and a wizard when it comes to crafting airtight prenuptial agreements. It's a field that demands a deep understanding of the law, coupled with a keen ability to apply it with empathy and sensitivity.But the true reward of a career in family and domestic relations law lies in the intense impact you can have on the lives of your clients. Imagine the joy of reuniting a parent with their child, the relief of securing financial stability for a client in the midst of a divorce, or the gratitude of a client who finally feels heard and understood after years of domestic turmoil.

It's a path that requires a special kind of person – one who can balance the emotional weight of the work with the intellectual rigor of the law. It's a calling for those who are willing to wade into the messiness of human relationships, to be the steady hand that guides families through their darkest moments, and to ultimately make a tangible difference in the lives of those they serve.

So, if you're ready to trade in your legal pads for a box of tissues and a heart full of empathy, then family and domestic relations law might just be the specialization that's calling your name. Brace yourself for the emotional roller coaster, but know that the rewards of this field are truly immeasurable.

Exploring Alternative Career Paths

Government and Public Service

So, you've conquered the private sector, eh? Well, how about a little adventure on the other side of the fence? Turns out, government and public service can be a veritable playground for lawyers looking to make a real impact. Forget those stuffy boardrooms and never ending client meetings – this is where the action is at.

Picture this: You, standing tall in a crisp suit, addressing a room full of policymakers and community leaders. Your words, sharper than a freshly honed katana, cut through the bureaucratic noise like a hot knife through butter. One moment, you're crafting legislation that could change the course of a city; the next, you're leading a team of passionate advocates, fighting for the rights of the underdogs. It's a thrill ride, my friend, and you're the driver.

But don't be fooled – this ain't no walk in the park. Navigating the political scene can be like wading through a minefield of egos and agendas. You'll need to be part strategist, part diplomat, and part Jedi mind trick master. But hey, if you can handle the pressure of a high stakes trial, this should be a piece of cake, right?

The rewards, though, are worth it. Imagine the satisfaction of seeing your hard work translate into real, tangible change – whether it's improving access to education, supporting environmental protection, or supporting the causes of the marginalized. It's the kind of legacy that makes you feel like you're truly making a difference, one case at a time.

In House Counsel

So, you've had your fill of the corporate grind, huh? Well, how about a little change of pace – say, becoming the legal mastermind behind the scenes? That's right, it's time to step out of the courtroom and into the boardroom, where the real power players reside.

As an in house counsel, you'll be the legal guardian angel of a company, shielding it from the endless pitfalls and traps that lurk in the business world. It's a high stakes game, my friend, where a single misstep could send the entire operation crashing down like a house of cards in a hurricane.

But don't worry, you're no stranger to pressure. In fact, you thrive on it. Whether it's negotiating a multi million-dollar merger, navigating the treacherous waters of intellectual property law, or crafting watertight contracts that could make a shark lawyer weep, you're the ninja of the legal world – swift, precise, and always one step ahead of the competition.

And the best part? You get to be a part of the inner workings of a company, shaping its very foundation and ensuring its success. It's like being a superstar quarterback, calling the plays and leading the team to victory. Plus, the perks ain't too shabby – corner office, anyone?

Of course, it's not all champagne and caviar. You'll need to be a master of adaptability, constantly learning and evolving to keep up with the ever changing business terrain. But hey, that's what keeps the job exciting, right? So, are you ready to trade in your courtroom attire for a seat at the big table?

Legal Consulting and Entrepreneurship

Ah, the siren call of entrepreneurship – the thrill of being your own boss, the endless possibilities, and the sweet, sweet freedom of not being chained to a desk for 80 hours a week. If that's the life you crave, my friend, then legal consulting and entrepreneurship might be the path for you.

Imagine this: You, the legal mastermind, releasing your expertise on the world, one client at a time. No more dealing with the corporate red tape, the office politics, or the soul crushing billable hours. Instead, you'll be the architect of your own destiny, crafting customized legal solutions for a diverse array of clients, from tech startups to Mom and-Pop shops.

And let's not forget the perks – the flexible schedule, the ability to work from anywhere with a decent Wi Fi connection, and the sheer joy of watching your own business grow and thrive. It's like being a superhero, swooping in to save the day with your sharp legal mind and your unparalleled problem solving skills.

Of course, it's not all sunshine and rainbows. Entrepreneurship comes with its own set of challenges – from drumming up a steady stream of clients to navigating the ever evolving situation of regulations and compliance. But hey, that's where your lawyer skills really shine, right? You're a master of research, analysis, and finding creative solutions to seemingly insurmountable problems.

So, are you ready to take the leap and join the ranks of the legal entrepreneurs? Just remember, the only limit is your own imagination. So, what are you waiting for? Go forth and conquer the world, one client at a time!

Overcoming Challenges and Setbacks

Dealing with Rejection and Failure

Rejection and failure - two words that can strike fear into the hearts of even the most seasoned lawyers. But let me tell you, my friend, these are the stepping stones to greatness. Embrace them, for they are the keys to uncovering your true potential.

When that dream job slips through your fingers or that big case doesn't go your way, it's easy to feel like the world is crashing down around you. But take a deep breath and remember this: failure is not the end, it's just the beginning of a new and even more exciting chapter.

Use that rejection as fuel to ignite your passion and drive. Channel your inner Rocky Balboa and come out swinging. Analyze what went wrong, learn from your mistakes, and come back stronger than ever. Failure is the greatest teacher you'll ever have, so treat it like the gift it truly is.

And when the self doubt creeps in, remember this: every successful lawyer has faced their fair share of setbacks. The ones who make it to the top are the ones who refused to give up, who embraced the chaos and turned it into their own personal playground.

Maintaining Resilience and Perseverance

Resilience and perseverance - the dynamic duo that will carry you through even the darkest of legal storms. When the going gets tough, and the stress starts to pile up, it's time to channel your inner superhero.

First and foremost, never, ever, ever give up. Quitting is for mere mortals, and you, my friend, are destined for greatness. Whenever the weight of the world starts to feel a little too heavy, take a step back, take a deep breath, and remind yourself of why you started this journey in the first place.

Embrace the chaos, the sleepless nights, the endless hours of research and writing. These are the battle scars that will forge you into the legal powerhouse you were born to be. Each challenge you overcome, each obstacle you conquer, is a proof to your unwavering resilience.

And remember, you're not alone in this fight. Reach out to your fellow legal warriors, your mentors, your support system. Lean on them when the going gets tough, and let them help you rediscover your inner strength. Together, you can weather any storm and emerge victorious.

Seeking Support and Mentorship

In the high stakes world of law, it's easy to feel like you're navigating a treacherous jungle all by yourself. But let me let you in on a little secret: you don't have to go it alone.

Seek out mentors, those seasoned legal veterans who have already blazed a trail through the wilderness. These experienced guides can offer indispensable understanding, sage advice, and a shoulder to lean on when the pressures of the job start to weigh you down.

But don't just settle for the first mentor who comes your way. Shop around, find someone whose values and experiences harmonize with your own. This isn't just about getting career advice – it's about building a meaningful connection, a true partnership that will help you overcome even the toughest challenges.

And remember, it's not just about what your mentor can do for you. Offer to lend a helping hand, volunteer for projects, or simply be a sounding board for their own struggles. A mutually beneficial mentorship is the secret sauce that will help you both reach new heights of success.

So, don't be afraid to reach out, to put yourself out there, to ask for help when you need it. In the legal world, we're all in this together, and with the right support system by your side, there's no obstacle you can't overcome.

Balancing Work and Personal Life

Effective Time Management

Ah, the elusive work life balance. It's the holy grail that every lawyer seems to be chasing, yet so few seem to catch. But fear not, my friend, for I'm about to let you in on a few secrets that'll have you juggling billable hours and personal time like a pro.

First things first, ditch the notion of "work life balance" altogether. That's a surefire recipe for disappointment and burnout. Instead, embrace the concept of "work life integration." Envision your professional and personal lives not as separate spheres, but as interwoven threads that create the rich blend of your existence. Trust me, it'll make that endless stream of client emails and court appearances a lot more bearable.

Now, let's talk about time management. Forget the rigid, minute by-minute schedules - those are for robot lawyers, not humans like you and me. Instead, adopt a flexible approach that allows you to seamlessly transition between tasks and responsibilities. Set broad goals, not narrow deadlines, and be willing to adjust on the fly. After all, who knows when inspiration will strike and you'll need to drop everything to jot down your next legal masterpiece?

And speaking of inspiration, don't be afraid to embrace the power of procrastination. That's right, I said it. Sometimes, the best way to tackle a daunting task is to let your mind wander, whether it's through a lunchtime stroll or a few rounds of desk chair spin offs. You never know when that eureka moment will hit, and it might just save you from burning the midnight oil.

Cultivating Hobbies and Interests

As lawyers, we often get so caught up in the hustle and bustle of our profession that we forget the simple joys of life outside the courtroom. But let me tell you, embracing your passions and interests is not just a way to unwind - it's a secret weapon for professional success.

Think about it - when was the last time you truly let your mind wander, free from the constraints of billable hours and legal strategies? That's where the magic happens, my friends. Whether it's painting, woodworking, or collecting rare Pokemon cards (no judgment here), diving into a hobby can do wonders for your mental clarity and problem solving skills.

But don't just take my word for it. Studies have shown that lawyers who engage in regular leisure activities are less likely to experience burnout and more likely to excel in their careers. So, go ahead and indulge in that guilty pleasure - I promise, your clients and partners won't mind if you show up to the next meeting with paint stained hands or a pocket full of Pikachu cards.

And let's not forget the social benefits of having a rich array of interests. Networking events can be tedious affairs, but imagine the conversation starting power of being able to regale your colleagues with tales of your latest pottery throwing mishap or your quest to catch the elusive shiny Charizard. Trust me, it'll set you apart from the sea of stuffy lawyers in suits and ties.

Maintaining Healthy Relationships

Now, let's talk about the most important aspect of work life balance: your relationships. Because let's be honest, what good is all that billable time and client development if you don't have anyone to share it with?

It's easy to get caught up in the rat race, prioritizing professional advancement over personal connections. But trust me, your loved ones - whether it's your significant other, your family, or your closest friends - are the true foundation of a fulfilling life. And don't worry, I'm not going to lecture you on the virtues of quality time and emotional support. I know you're a lawyer, not a relationship guru.

Instead, let me offer you a few practical tips. First and foremost, learn to set boundaries. It's okay to say no to that last minute client call or weekend work session. Your loved ones deserve your undivided attention, and trust me, they'll thank you for it (even if they don't show it at the time).

And when you do get that precious time together, make it count. Ditch the phone, turn off the TV, and truly engage. Whether it's a candlelit dinner with your partner or a game night with your closest friends, those moments of genuine connection will nourish your soul in ways you never thought possible.

Remember, your career may be the vehicle that gets you to

the top, but your relationships are the roadmap that guides you there. So, treat them with the care and attention they deserve, and watch as your personal and professional lives blossom in perfect harmony.

Giving Back to the Community

Pro Bono Work and Volunteer Opportunities

As lawyers, we have a unique opportunity to make a lasting impact on our communities. And let's be real, the legal profession isn't exactly known for its altruism. But fear not, my fellow counselors – there's a way to balance that billable hour hustle with a healthy dose of do gooding. It's called pro bono work, and it's the secret sauce to keeping your soul intact while climbing that corporate ladder.

Sure, you could spend your evenings binge watching the latest true crime docuseries, but why not put those legal superpowers to good use? Whether it's helping low income families navigate the byzantine world of housing laws, or providing free legal representation to non profit organizations, pro bono work is the ultimate win win. You get to flex your lawyerly muscles, and the less fortunate get the justice they deserve. Plus, let's be honest – when was the last time your colleagues at the firm actually impressed anyone by their Netflix viewing habits?

But pro bono isn't the only way to give back. Volunteering your time and expertise can be equally rewarding. From serving on the board of a local charity to leading legal workshops in underserved communities, there are endless opportunities to make a difference. Just be sure to choose causes that truly appeal with you – that way, you'll be more invested in the work and less tempted to use the "billable hours" excuse to wiggle out of your commitments.

And let's not forget the networking potential. When you step outside the ivory tower of your law firm, you never know who you might meet. That pro bono client could turn out to be a well connected mover and shaker, or that community legal clinic might introduce you to your next dream job. Think of it as a win win-win scenario: you get to do good, feel good, and potentially advance your career in the process. Now, who said being a lawyer had to be all about the Benjamins?

Participating in Bar Associations

Ah, the bar association – that hallowed ground where lawyers gather to debate the finer points of tort law and network like their lives depend on it. Sure, it might seem like a stuffy, old school institution, but trust me, there's a lot of power in those stuffy halls.

For starters, getting involved in your local bar association is a surefire way to raise your profile in the legal community. Volunteer for a committee, run for a leadership position, or organize a continuing education event. Not only will you be rubbing elbows with the movers and shakers of the legal world, but you'll also be positioning yourself as an expert in your field. And let's be real, who doesn't love a good ol' fashioned power play?

But the benefits of bar association involvement go beyond just personal gain. These organizations are often at the forefront of advocating for important legal issues, from judicial appointments to legislative reform. By lending your voice and expertise, you can help shape the future of the legal profession and make a real impact on the lives of your fellow citizens.

And let's not forget the networking opportunities. Sure, the annual gala might feel like a scene straight out of "Suits," but trust me, those stuffy old lawyers know a thing or two about making connections. You never know when that casual conversation over a glass of subpar pinot noir might lead to your next big client or career changing opportunity.

So, don't be afraid to dive headfirst into the world of bar associations. Just remember to keep your sense of humor and your wits about you – after all, you're dealing with a room full of lawyers. But if you can navigate those treacherous waters, the rewards can be truly impressive.

Mentoring and Educating Future Lawyers

As seasoned lawyers, we have a responsibility to pay it forward and nurture the next generation of legal eagles. And no, I'm not talking about those tedious lunch and-learn sessions where you drone on about the finer points of contract law. I'm talking about getting your hands dirty and truly investing in the future of the profession.

Mentoring young lawyers or law students can be one of the most rewarding experiences of your career. Think about the challenges you faced when you were first starting out – the imposter syndrome, the imposing partners, the sheer terror of appearing in court for the first time. Now, imagine having a seasoned professional in your corner, guiding you through those treacherous waters. That's the power of mentorship, and it's a gift that keeps on giving.

But it's not just about sharing your hard earned wisdom and experience. Mentoring is also about learning from the next generation of legal minds. These young go getters are brimming with fresh ideas, new approaches, and a healthy disregard for the status quo. By opening yourself up to their perspectives, you can breathe new life into your own practice and stay ahead of the curve in a constantly evolving profession.

And let's not forget the educational side of things. Whether it's guest lecturing at your alma mater, leading a continuing education seminar, or developing a summer internship program, the opportunity to shape the minds of future lawyers is a privilege not to be taken lightly. After all, who better to teach the art of courtroom dramatics than a seasoned pro who's been in the trenches, battling it out with the best of them?

So, if you're looking to leave a lasting legacy and ensure the legal profession remains in capable hands, don't hesitate to get involved in mentoring and education. Trust me, the rewards - both personal and professional - will far outweigh the time and effort you invest. And who knows, you might just discover your inner teacher lurking beneath that formidable lawyer facade.

Adapting to a Changing Legal Terrain

Technological Advancements in the Legal Field

In the ever evolving world of law, keeping up with technological advancements is no longer an option - it's a necessity. Gone are the days when lawyers could simply rely on dusty tomes and a trusty typewriter. Today, the legal profession is abuzz with a dizzying array of digital tools and platforms that are transforming the way we practice, communicate, and deliver results for our clients.

Embrace the power of artificial intelligence, my friend. AI powered legal research platforms can now sift through mountains of case law and precedents in a matter of seconds, freeing up precious time for more strategic and creative tasks. Don't be that dinosaur who still spends hours manually poring over dusty law journals - be the legal eagle who soars above the competition with the help of cutting edge technology.

And speaking of communication, let's not forget the impact of video conferencing and cloud based collaboration tools. Gone are the days of endless meetings and chaotic email threads. Now, you can gather your legal team from across the globe, hash out strategies in real time, and seamlessly share documents - all with the click of a button. It's like having a virtual law firm in the palm of your hand, complete with a revolving door of coffee refills and witty banter.

But the technological revolution doesn't stop there. Blockchain, cryptocurrency, and smart contracts are reshaping the legal scene, introducing new challenges and opportunities for savvy practitioners. Imagine being the lawyer who can navigate the murky waters of digital asset management or draft airtight smart contracts that leave no room for loopholes. You'll be the talk of the town, my friend, the one everyone turns to when the digital world collides with the world of law.

Emerging Areas of Law and Practice

As the world evolves, so too must the legal profession. And with this change comes a wealth of new and exciting areas of law and practice, just waiting to be explored. So, put on your adventurer's hat and get ready to venture into the unknown.

First up, the captivating realm of cybersecurity and data privacy. With the exponential growth of digital technology, the need for lawyers who can navigate the complex web of data protection regulations and tackle the ever evolving threats of cybercrime has never been greater. Imagine being the legal guardian who safeguards the digital assets and privacy of your clients, shielding them from the dark corners of the internet with your razor sharp legal expertise.

But that's just the tip of the iceberg. As our world becomes more interconnected, the field of international and cross border law is experiencing a surge in demand. Whether it's guiding clients through the intricacies of international trade agreements, navigating the labyrinth of global taxation, or representing parties in high stakes international disputes, the possibilities are endless for the lawyer who's willing to embrace the global stage.

And let's not forget the ever evolving scene of intellectual property law. In the age of digital innovation, protecting the ideas and creations of our clients has become a veritable minefield. But for the savvy lawyer who can untangle the complexities of patents, copyrights, and trademarks, the rewards are plentiful. Imagine being the legal mastermind who helps cutting edge startups and visionary entrepreneurs safeguard their most valuable assets - their ideas.

Continuous Learning and Adaptation

In a world that's in a constant state of flux, the most successful lawyers are those who embrace the power of continuous learning and adaptation. Gone are the days when a single law degree and a decade of experience were enough to coast through a legal career. Today, the legal scene is a rapidly evolving beast, and the only way to tame it is to never stop learning, growing, and adapting.

Start by immersing yourself in the latest legal trends, technologies, and industry developments. Attend conferences, join professional associations, and follow is an influencer in your field. Be the legal eagle who's always ahead of the curve, ready to pounce on the next big opportunity before the competition even knows it exists.

But learning doesn't stop there, my friend. Embrace the power of continuous self improvement. Sharpen your writing skills, hone your public speaking abilities, and master the art of negotiation. Become the lawyer who's not just a legal expert, but a versatile problem solver, a captivating storyteller, and a master of persuasion.

And don't forget to step outside your comfort zone. Venture into new areas of practice, explore emerging fields of law, or even consider a career adjust. The legal profession is a vast and varied situation, and the more you're willing to explore it, the more opportunities will present themselves. Who knows, maybe you'll discover a niche that's tailor made for your unique talents and passions.

Remember, the legal world is constantly evolving, and the lawyers who thrive in this ever changing terrain are the ones who are willing to adapt, learn, and grow. So, embrace the challenge, my friend, and let your legal career soar to new heights.

Leaving a Lasting Legacy

Reflections on a Rewarding Career

As you reach the pinnacle of your legal career, take a moment to reflect on the journey that has brought you here. The path has been far from easy, with its fair share of twists and turns, but looking back, you can't help but feel a intense sense of pride and accomplishment. The countless hours spent poring over textbooks, the nerve wracking exam days, and the steep learning curves of those early years in the profession – it's all been worth it.

Remember the first time you stepped into a courtroom, your heart pounding with a mix of excitement and trepidation? Those early victories, when you managed to sway the judge or impress a client, were the fuel that kept you going, propelling you forward even when the challenges seemed insurmountable. And now, as you stand at the top of your game, you can't help but marvel at how far you've come.

The legal field has evolved significantly during your career, and you've had a front row seat to the changes – from the rise of technology in the industry to the shifting societal attitudes toward the role of lawyers. Through it all, you've remained steadfast, adapting and innovating, always seeking to stay ahead of the curve. Your colleagues and clients have come to rely on your expertise, your unwavering commitment, and your unparalleled problem solving skills.

But beyond the accolades and the successes, what truly fills your heart with a deep sense of satisfaction is the positive impact you've had on the lives of your clients. Whether it was securing a essential settlement, navigating a complex regulatory terrain, or advocating for the rights of the underserved, you've made a tangible difference in the world. And that, my friend, is the true measure of a rewarding career.

Passing on Knowledge and Wisdom

As you approach the twilight of your legal career, you find yourself in a unique position - one where your decades of experience and accumulated wisdom have become priceless assets. It's time to share what you've learned, to mentor and inspire the next generation of legal professionals.

Remember that eager young associate who joined your firm, fresh faced and bursting with enthusiasm? Well, it's your turn to be that guiding light, to share the lessons you've learned the hard way and to help them navigate the treacherous waters of the legal setting. Whether it's offering advice on managing a heavy caseload, navigating the delicate art of client relationships, or weathering the storms of professional setbacks, your wisdom can be the difference between a thriving career and a burnout induced disaster.

But your mentorship role extends beyond the walls of your firm. You can lend your expertise to law schools, offering guest lectures, participating in mock trials, and providing realizations into the realities of legal practice. By sharing your experiences, both triumphs, and tribulations, you can inspire and enable the future leaders of the legal profession, instilling in them the courage and resilience to tackle the challenges that lie ahead.

And let's not forget about your peers – the seasoned veterans who are treading the same path. Organize networking events, help round table discussions, and create a supportive community where knowledge and effective techniques can be freely exchanged. After all, the legal field is a mixture woven with the collective experiences of those who have come before, and it's up to you to ensure that this rich heritage is preserved and passed on.

Retirement and Transition Planning

As you approach the end of your storied legal career, the idea of retirement may bring a mix of emotions – excitement, trepidation, and perhaps even a touch of uncertainty. After decades of dedicating yourself to the profession, the thought of stepping away can be both liberating and daunting.

But fear not, for with a well crafted transition plan, you can begin on this next chapter of your life with confidence and enthusiasm. Start by taking a long, hard look at your financial portfolio – have you saved enough to maintain your lifestyle and explore the new horizons that retirement promises? Consult with financial advisors, crunch the numbers, and ensure that your golden years will be truly golden.

As you envision your post retirement life, don't forget to consider the non financial aspects as well. What hobbies or passions have you put on the backburner over the years? Now is the time to dust them off and give them the attention they deserve. Whether it's reconnecting with old friends, traveling to exotic destinations, or diving into a long neglected creative pursuit, this is your opportunity to redefine your identity and live life on your own terms.

But don't completely sever your ties with the legal world just yet. Many seasoned lawyers find fulfillment in continuing to contribute to the profession in a more limited capacity, perhaps by serving on boards, acting as consultants, or even teaching. This not only keeps your mind sharp but also allows you to leave a lasting legacy, inspiring and guiding the next generation of legal professionals.

As you begin on this new chapter, remember to embrace the uncertainty and the excitement. After all, you've earned the right to write your own story, to explore the world beyond the confines of the courtroom. So, take a deep breath, savor the memories of your illustrious career, and get ready to start on the next adventure.

Copyright 2024

Silas Meadowlark

www.ingramcontent.com/pod-product-compliance
Lightning Source LLC
Chambersburg PA
CBHW030503220526
45464CB00006B/2641